Americans All biographies are inspiring life stories about people of all races, creeds, and nationalities who have uniquely contributed to the American way of life. Highlights from each person's story develop his contributions in his special field — whether they be in the arts, industry, human rights, education, science and medicine, or sports.

Specific abilities, character, and accomplishments are emphasized. Often despite great odds, these famous people have attained success in their fields through the good use of ability, determination, and hard work. These fast-moving stories of real people will show the way to better understanding of the ingredients necessary for personal success.

Henry Ford and his first automobile in 1896

Henry Ford

AUTOMOTIVE PIONEER

by Elizabeth Rider Montgomery

illustrated by Russell Hoover

GARRARD PUBLISHING COMPANY
CHAMPAIGN. ILLINOIS

For Bruce Phillips

J
920
F

Picture credits:

Ford Archives, Henry Ford Museum, Dearborn, Michigan: p. 2, 28(both), 36, 52, 65(both), 66, 80, 83, 94

Contents

1. The Tinkerer

Nine-year-old Henry Ford stood in the kitchen of his parents' farmhouse near Dearborn, Michigan. He stared at the steaming teakettle on the big black range. It was the year 1872.

"What makes steam?" Henry asked.

His mother was busy cooking. She had a family of eight to feed, besides several farm hands and the schoolteacher who boarded there.

"When water gets hot, it turns into steam," she replied.

"What would happen," the boy wondered, "if I plugged up the spout?"

He knew he would be scolded if he experimented with the teakettle, so instead he filled a jug with water. He corked it tightly and set it on the hottest part of the stove.

Soon the jug burst into fragments. One of them hit Henry's head and cut it. Water sputtered on the hot stove and splattered onto the kitchen floor. Without a word of complaint Mrs. Ford wiped it up. She understood her son had to find out for himself how everything worked.

As Henry mopped at the blood streaming down his face, he smiled ruefully at his mother. He had discovered the power of steam.

Most of Henry's spare time was spent in experimenting and tinkering. But a farmer's boy had little spare time, for even the smallest of the children had chores to do. Henry chopped kindling, kept the kitchen and sitting-room wood-boxes full, and carried water from the well. Each night he brought the cows back from the fields where they had grazed during the day.

As Henry grew older, he cared for the horses as well as the cows, and he helped with milking, plowing, planting, haying, and harvesting. By the time he was twelve, Henry was doing a man's work. His younger brother, John, had taken over his earlier chores. Margaret and Jane, the older girls of the family, helped their mother with the housework.

Usually Henry worked cheerfully and

well, but he longed for machines that would lighten the heavy farm work. He wanted to have more time for playing, bird-watching, and tinkering.

Mr. Ford didn't think much of Henry's tinkering when the boy made such things as a water wheel that would grind clay and potatoes, or a forge in which bits of broken glass could be melted. But when Henry repaired a harness, reset a tool handle, or made some hinges for furniture, Henry's father was pleased. These activities saved money. Mr. Ford was not pleased, however, when his son repaired things for neighbors, as he often did, without charging them a cent.

Henry set up a workbench in front of the window in his attic bedroom. There he worked evening after evening on the machinery brought to him for repair.

Mostly he used tools he made himself from nails, knitting needles, and pieces of steel. In winter he set a lighted lantern on the floor beside his feet to keep them warm.

The year Henry was twelve someone gave him a watch, and he promptly took it apart to see how it worked. After many trials he assembled the watch again, and it ran as well as ever. After that he repaired every watch and every clock he could get his hands on. A neighbor remarked jokingly, "The clocks all shudder when they see Henry Ford coming!" And Henry's brothers and sisters warned each other to keep toys out of Henry's sight. He was sure to take them apart to see how they were made.

2. Good–bye to the Farm

In March, 1876, when Henry was nearly thirteen, his mother died. Mr. Ford's sister, Mrs. Rebecca Flaherty, came to the farm to keep house, but Henry missed his mother.

As Mrs. Ford had done, Mrs. Flaherty did all the family washing, helped by Margaret and Jane. They scrubbed the clothes by hand on a washboard and ironed with heavy irons heated on the kitchen stove. They cleaned house with broom, dustpan, and dustcloth. They churned butter, made candles and soap, and baked all the bread, cakes, and pies the family ate. They canned fruit, made jams, jellies, and pickles, and helped smoke hams and bacon. They fed the chickens, cared for the vegetable garden, did the mending, and knitted stockings and mittens. They also made the family's clothing on a treadle sewing machine, which was worked by pumping a pedal to turn the wheels.

After a short time Mrs. Flaherty left, and her daughter Jane Flaherty came to take charge of the household.

The house was kept clean, the meals were served on time, and the clothes were kept in order. But Henry was no longer happy. Without his mother the house did not seem like home.

"It's like a watch without a main-spring," Henry thought. Sometimes he "fiddled" on an old violin to cheer himself up.

In July of that year something exciting happened. As Henry was riding to town beside his father on the wagon, he saw a steam engine moving under its own power! He had seen steam engines before. Farmers used them to operate threshing machines and sawmills, but always the engines were hauled by horses.

This strange machine frightened the Fords' horses. The engine driver stopped to let them pass. Henry jumped from the high wagon seat and ran to the steam engine.

"What makes it run?" he asked eagerly.

The friendly driver, standing on a platform behind the boiler, smiled at the boy's

excitement. He showed him the different parts of the machine: engine and boiler mounted on wheels, with water tank and coal cart trailing behind. He demonstrated how he shoveled coal to build up steam in the boiler. He pointed out the chain that connected the engine to the rear wheels and made them turn, and the pulley that could be attached to thresher or sawmill to provide power.

"How fast does the engine go?" Henry asked.

"It makes 200 revolutions a minute," the driver answered. Henry understood that meant the engine turned over 200 times each minute.

Mr. Ford had to call Henry half a dozen times before he could pry him away from the fascinating engine.

"Someday," Henry thought as he climbed

back on the wagon seat, "I'll make a carriage that will travel without horses."

Henry stayed on the farm for three more years, but he disliked farm work more and more. Each day he walked three miles to the ungraded rural school. He was a fairly good student. He enjoyed memorizing poems from the McGuffey Readers, but he disliked the daily spelling lesson. He liked arithmetic best of all.

When Henry was sixteen he finished his studies at the district school. Then he announced, "I'm going to Detroit. I'll get a job where I can learn about engines and machinery."

His father objected, but Henry was determined to go. Finally in December he hung his violin on a hook in the barn, packed up his clothes and his tools, and walked to Detroit, ten miles away.

3. In the Big City

Detroit, with its 100,000 people, was noisy and exciting. Horses filled the streets, pulling buggies, carriages, wagons, streetcars, and buses. Some streets were paved with tarred cedar blocks, and some with cobblestones. Most streets, however, were nothing but dirt that became thick mud in winter and deep dust in summer.

Henry was impressed by the city's gas street lights and that marvelous new invention the telephone. But the pipes that brought water right into Detroit

houses seemed to him most wonderful of all. Imagine not having to carry water from a well! On the farm he had longed for such labor-saving devices.

Henry's first job with the Michigan Car Company did not last long.

He soon started work at James Flower & Brothers' Machine Shop. The wages were only $2.50 a week for eleven hours of work each day, and he had to pay

$3.50 a week for board and room. So he got an evening job at Magill's Jewelry Shop, for $2 each week, cleaning and winding the shop's large stock of clocks. Six days every week Henry worked as apprentice at the machine shop, and six nights a week he worked on clocks.

At first he merely cleaned and wound the clocks, but soon he was repairing them also. Then he started in on watches.

Mr. Magill would not let Henry work at the front workbench, because customers might object if they saw a young boy taking their valuable watches and clocks apart. So he put Henry in the back room out of sight. Henry didn't care, so long as he was working on machinery.

Watches were expensive in those days because the manufacturing was largely handwork. Henry had a plan for making a low-priced watch, doing most of the labor through the use of machinery. He told his idea to a young jeweler he met in Magill's Jewelry Shop.

"If watches could be made in large quantities," Henry said, "they could be sold cheaply. All parts could be made by machinery so they would fit any watch. If I could make 2,000 watches a day I could afford to sell them at thirty cents apiece. And I'd still make enough money."

Henry's plans interested the young jeweler. "Why don't we go into business together?" he suggested. "You make the models for the machines and the parts, and I'll cut the dies."

So Henry began preparations for starting a watch factory. Late at night he toiled at the workbench he had clamped onto the windowsill of his rented room. Soon the teacher in the adjoining room complained that the noise of Henry's tools set her teeth on edge. The landlord told Henry the work had to stop.

Henry didn't really mind quitting. He had already decided to drop the project, because he didn't think he could ever sell 2,000 watches a day. Not everybody wanted a watch. He'd have to make something everybody wanted.

4. Back to the Farm

Henry took a new job with the Detroit Dry Dock Company so that he could learn more about different kinds of engines. Mr. Ford still couldn't understand his son's passion for machinery. He never gave up trying to persuade Henry to return to the farm. Finally, after Henry had been in Detroit almost three years, he agreed to go home.

Nineteen-year-old Henry found routine farm work no more appealing than he had when he was younger. But he did enjoy the birds and the wildlife in the country, and he liked operating and repairing a steam threshing machine. That summer he took it around the countryside, from one farm to another. He also sold and serviced portable steam engines throughout the state of Michigan.

Margaret was old enough now to run the house, and she had taken the place of their cousin, Jane Flaherty. Margaret taught her brother to dance so they could go to the country square dances together.

At a dance on New Year's Eve in 1885, Henry danced with a dark-haired girl, Clara Bryant, who lived a few miles away. He had met Clara briefly the year before.

"Would you like to see a watch I made?" Henry asked when they stopped to rest after a fast-whirling dance.

"Why, yes," Clara replied. She was very surprised when she saw Henry's watch, because it had two sets of hands.

"One set is for sun time," Henry explained, "and the other for railroad time."

Clara didn't understand the difference. She enjoyed books and music, cooking and sewing, but she knew nothing about

mechanics. However, she was impressed, and when she got home she told her parents about the sensible, serious-minded young man she had met.

After that Clara often went bobsledding and ice skating with Henry. That summer they attended picnics, strawberry festivals, hay rides, and corn huskings. When Mr. Ford saw that Henry was thinking of getting married, he gave him 40 acres of wooded land. A small cottage, which would serve as a temporary home, stood on the land.

In 1888 Henry and Clara were married. In their new home they arranged all of the curtains, rugs, and quilts that Clara had made, and they were ready to start housekeeping.

Henry fitted out a sawmill and a portable steam engine. He cut the timber

These photographs of Clara and Henry are considered to be their wedding pictures.

on his land and sawed it into lumber. He used some of the lumber to build a new house, and he sold the rest.

The young couple was very content. When Henry came home from work, he would whistle one phrase of a familiar tune. Clara would reply with the next phrase as she ran to meet him. In the evenings Clara often read aloud to her

28

husband, or she played the small reed organ he bought her. Occasionally Henry fiddled an accompaniment.

Mr. Ford now thought that Henry was settled for life. Clara was not so sure. Henry spent much of his spare time experimenting with engines. He made a steam road engine, but it didn't work very well. It was too heavy, he decided.

One day, when Clara and Henry had been married for more than three years, Henry saw an internal-combustion gas engine in Detroit.

He told Clara about it that evening as she played her organ. "That's the kind of motor I need for my road engine. It doesn't need a boiler, and it doesn't need steam."

He reached up to the organ and took down a sheet of Clara's music. On the back he sketched his idea for a horseless-carriage engine.

"It would work, Callie," he said. "I'm sure of it."

Clara encouraged him. "Go ahead and make it."

"I'd need special tools and materials," Henry objected. "I can't get them out here in the country. To make a gas engine, I would have to move to Detroit and take that job the Edison Illuminating Company offered me."

Clara looked around their home, the little house Henry had built for her. She loved every corner of it. She liked living near her parents. She even liked living on a farm, because she had never known any other life. But if Henry wanted to go to Detroit, they must surely go.

"When shall we move?" she asked.

5. The Horseless Carriage

For two years Henry worked nights as a steam engineer for the Edison Illuminating Company. He worked every night from 6 P.M. to 6 A.M. and earned $45 a month. After working hours he experimented on his gas engine. His wages barely paid for living expenses and for tools and materials for his tinkering. But Clara never complained, because Henry was happy.

In November, 1893, a son was born to Henry and Clara. A few weeks later the young Fords moved into a double house at 58 Bagley Avenue. While Clara took care of little Edsel and arranged furniture, Henry set up a workshop in the Fords' half of the small brick shed behind the house. Then he began to work in earnest on his gasoline engine.

On Christmas Eve Clara was almost ready to rest after a busy day preparing for the next day's company dinner. Just as she had gotten the baby settled down to sleep, the kitchen door opened and Henry came in. He carried a strange object made of such things as gas pipe, an old crankshaft, and a makeshift flywheel.

"Help me try out my engine, will you, Callie?" he asked.

"What shall I do?" Clara inquired.

"Just feed the gasoline into the motor," Henry answered. He clamped the engine to the kitchen sink. Then he fastened a wire from the engine's spark plug to the light socket that hung from the ceiling of the room. He attached another wire from the engine to one of the water pipes at the sink.

Then Henry handed Clara an oilcan of gasoline and showed her how to drip it into a metal cup which acted as a carburetor. As she poured, she turned a screw so that the gasoline would feed into the intake valve.

"Now," Henry said, "when I turn the flywheel, air and gas will be sucked into the cylinder, and the motor should start."

Soon the engine began to run. The kitchen light flickered wildly. Flames shot out of the engine's exhaust pipe.

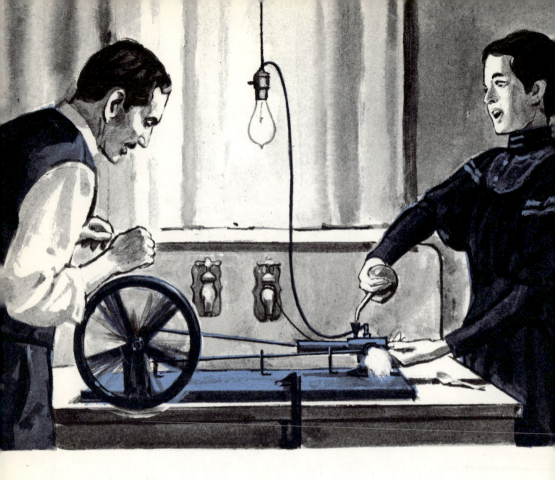

The vibration of the motor shook the sink and even the kitchen. Clara shivered with excitement and a bit of fear, but Henry smiled happily.

"It works!" he exclaimed, shutting off the engine. "Now I'll build a bigger one, a motor with two cylinders. I'll start on it tomorrow."

34

"Oh, no, Henry!" Clara protested. "To-morrow is Christmas Day. My folks are coming for dinner."

"All right," Henry replied. "I'll wait until the next day."

For two and a half years Henry spent every spare moment working on his gas engines. He soon got higher wages and better working hours at the Edison Illuminating Company, because his employers had discovered that he was an excellent mechanic with steam engines and dynamos. He was earning enough money now to buy a bicycle.

Riding bicycles had become popular. Women now wore short skirts, just above the ankle, so that they could ride more easily.

When Henry completed his two-cylinder engine, he tried to attach it to a bicycle.

It didn't work, so he built a four-wheeled carriage for it, using bicycle wheels. A tiller was attached to the front wheels for steering. The driver would sit on a bicycle saddle fastened on top of a three-gallon gas tank.

Henry knew that other men, including Duryea, Haynes, Olds, and Winton, had

Henry's first bicycle. Later, he said that it was as easy to run a car as a bicycle.

built horseless carriages, but he had never seen any and he knew none of the details of the others' work. He used his own ideas.

At night Clara always waited up for Henry. Usually she had some hot milk ready for him, when he finally quit work in his shop.

One rainy June night in 1896, Clara waited and waited, but Henry did not come in. Suddenly, at about 2 A.M., she heard a tremendous noise behind their house. It sounded as if somebody were tearing the house down!

After an anxious look at the baby, Clara snatched up an umbrella and ran out of the back door. Somebody *was* tearing the house down. Henry was breaking out the back wall of the brick shed.

"What on earth are you doing?" Clara asked.

"I'm ready to try out my horseless carriage," Henry told Clara, lowering the sledge hammer. "But it's too big to go through the door."

Holding her umbrella, Clara watched Henry and his helper make the shed opening large enough for the carriage. Then Henry cranked the engine. When it started, he climbed on the bicycle saddle. He pulled back the lever that put the engine in low gear, and the carriage began to move. Engine sputtering, carriage vibrating, Henry jouncing up and down, the horseless carriage moved out of the shed into the alley and then onto the rough cobblestones of Grand River Avenue. The helper rode ahead of Henry on his bicycle to warn drivers of skittish horses. The car had no brakes, and no reverse gear, but Henry did not seem worried.

Clara stood in the rain watching until they turned the corner. She longed to follow, but she wouldn't leave the baby alone.

It seemed a long time before they returned. Henry was tired but triumphant.

"It works, Callie," he told her, as if she didn't know. "A small part dropped off and I had to go over to the Edison plant and make a new one. But the carriage runs. We went clear around the block."

"Now perhaps you can get some sleep," Clara replied.

6. The Big Step

Henry's horseless carriage excited great curiosity in Detroit. If it stalled when Henry was out driving, he couldn't leave it unguarded while he went for new parts or tools. Somebody was sure to remove some parts, or try to start the engine, or even carry the whole carriage away. So Henry kept a chain and lock with him, and he fastened the horseless carriage to a lamppost or a tree when he had to

leave it. Whenever he drove his carriage, someone had to ride ahead on a bicycle and warn drivers to hold their horses. Otherwise the animals might bolt and run away.

Henry's neighbors thought him a bit silly to be fooling with a toy like a horseless carriage. But Henry didn't care what other people thought, as long as

Clara believed in him. He called her the "Great Believer."

Then, in August of 1896, Henry received encouragement from someone else who mattered. The Edison Illuminating Company sent him to New York, to an electricians' convention. There, at a dinner, he met Thomas A. Edison, the most distinguished inventor of the day.

Alex Dow, Henry's boss, pointed Ford out to Edison. "That young man," he said, "has built a gasoline car. He thinks gas carriages will be more successful than electrical ones. He's wrong, of course, but I can't convince him."

Edison invited Ford to sit near him, and he began to ask questions. Ford drew a sketch of his mechanism on the back of a menu.

Suddenly Edison banged his fist on the table and the dishes jumped. "Young man," he declared, "you have something. Your car carries its own power plant. Keep at it!"

Henry returned to Detroit tremendously encouraged. He began at once to build a second horseless carriage.

Three years later the Detroit Automobile Company was formed. It planned to

build cars according to Henry Ford's design. He was offered the job of chief
engineer.

Alex Dow tried to persuade Henry to
turn down the offer. "Gasoline cars will
never be as dependable as electrical
cars," he insisted. "You're barking up
the wrong tree with your gas engine.
Besides, Henry, we want you as general
superintendent of the Edison Company

soon. But you can't have that job and carry on your work with the horseless-carriage too."

Henry reported this conversation to Clara. "What do you think, Callie?" he finished.

"Think?" she repeated. "I don't think, Henry. I *know*. You can't give up your horseless carriage. It's bound to be a big success very soon."

Henry felt the same way. So, even though he had a wife and a son to support, and very little money in the bank, he quit his job at the Edison Illuminating Company on August 15, 1899, just ten days after the new Detroit Automobile Company was established. Henry was thirty-six years old.

When his father heard the news, he was certain that Henry had lost his mind.

7. Henry Ford Fails Twice

Nothing went the way the members of the new company expected. Henry Ford would not permit the manufacture of a car until he was satisfied with his design. He kept on improving each part, especially the "mixer," or carburetor. A great deal of money was spent on experimental models, but they had not produced any cars for sale. In little more than a year, the Detroit Automobile Company failed.

Henry rented a loft and kept experimenting. Soon he built a racing car.

"If I could win a race," Henry told Clara, "I could get backers and form my own company."

In October, 1901, Ford entered his new car in a race at Grosse Point, not far from Detroit. Two other cars entered, but one dropped out because of a cylinder leak. The race was to be between Ford and Alexander Winton, who had already won several automobile races.

With 8,000 other people Clara and seven-year-old Edsel watched. Clara admitted to herself that Winton's 70-horsepower car did look very impressive. Henry's little 26-horsepower car didn't look like much, but she was sure it could run faster. It had to!

The starting gun sounded. The cars took off. At once Winton seized a big lead. Ford, not nearly so experienced in

racing, did not dare take chances. At the turns he shut off his power entirely. Much of the time his car was merely coasting.

Suddenly young Edsel shouted, "Look, Mamma! The other car is on fire!"

A big cloud of smoke billowed from the rear of Winton's machine. Henry sped past Winton as if the other car were standing still. He gained a bigger and bigger lead. By the time he finished the ten-mile course, he was three-fourths of a mile ahead. Clara and Edsel cheered themselves hoarse.

They greeted the winner rapturously. He was a frightful sight, with his clothes caked with mud and covered with oil. But he had won!

As Ford predicted, after winning the race he had no trouble getting backers.

In November, 1901, the Henry Ford Company was formed.

Unfortunately the new company fared no better than the first one. Ford wanted to build a low-priced car that ordinary people could afford to buy and drive. Other members of the company objected.

"It would be a waste of money to build a low-priced car," they said. "Wealthy people won't buy a cheap car, and poor people can't afford to buy any car."

In four months the company disbanded. Henry Ford had failed again.

He wasn't discouraged, however. He built another racing car, won another race, and then in June, 1903, a third company, the Ford Motor Company, was incorporated.

Within a few months it produced a two-cylinder, eight-horsepower car that

Edsel, at twelve, knew how to drive when
he and Henry posed in a Model F.

could go 30 miles an hour at top speed.
Like all cars of the period, it had no
doors, no top, and, of course, no self-
starter. Orders for the new car began to
come in faster than the Ford Motor Company could fill them. Most of the parts
were made in the Dodge Brothers' machine shop. They were loaded onto hay

52

wagons and delivered to the Ford assembly shop, where the wheels and body were attached and the automobile was painted.

Soon the Ford Motor Company built its own factory. For several years it experimented with models of varying prices. Each car was known by a model number. Model N, the best of the inexpensive cars, sold very well indeed. Ford became more and more convinced that the great market for automobiles lay in the low-priced field.

Except for James Couzens, the business manager, the rest of the directors disagreed. So Ford and Couzens began to buy out the other stockholders. Soon Ford owned a controlling interest in the Ford Motor Company. Now, he thought, he could do as he pleased.

8. "The Little Ford
Rambled Right Along"

One morning in early 1907, Henry Ford
and his head patternmaker, Charles Sorensen, met in a small locked room
in the Ford factory. The room contained
nothing but a table, a few power tools,
two big blackboards, and a rocking chair.

"Now, Charlie," Ford said, "we're ready
to start planning my universal car, a car
for the multitude. It must be cheap, so
that anybody can afford it. It must be
strong and tough, so it can go on any

kind of road. It must be simple, so an average man can keep it in repair."

"That's a large order," Sorensen said.

"We can do it," Ford insisted. "And when we come up with the right design, we'll build only one model. All our cars will be as much alike as pins or matches. We'll make thousands and sell them cheaply. The horse will disappear from the streets and highways, and the automobile will take its place."

Sorensen listened attentively. He made a few sketches and then a wooden model.

That was only the beginning. For a full year Sorensen and a few helpers worked in the secret room. Drawing after drawing was made, then came blueprints, models, and metal castings.

Ford dropped in often. He sat in the rocking chair and watched. Sometimes he

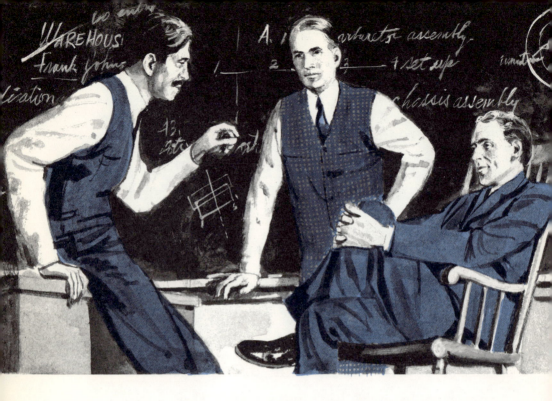

shook his head and made suggestions. Then the planners started over. Sometimes his smile flashed and he nodded approval.

"Charlie," he said one day, "we're on the right track. This new vanadium steel will make our car light but strong."

At last the plans of Ford's "universal car" were approved. The car, known as the Model T, went into production at the big new factory at Highland Park, near Detroit. A huge electric sign was placed on top of Detroit's Temple Theatre. Underneath the slogan, "Watch the Fords Go By" a Model T portrayed in lights seemed to move. Day after day crowds stood and watched the moving "car."

When the real Model T was displayed in October, 1908, public reaction varied.

"It's ugly," some people said. "It's just a black box on wheels."

"They've put the steering wheel on the left side," others objected. "It's always been on the right side."

"It will never run," declared a number of supposedly expert engineers. "That silly little car will fall apart when it gets out on the road."

But orders poured in. And when Model T's were delivered to buyers the following February, the new owners were delighted with them.

"Big automobiles get bogged down in the mud," one new Ford owner gloated. "But my little Ford rambles right along and quickly passes them up."

"My Ford gets 20 to 25 miles to a gallon of gas," boasted a farmer. "A neighbor, who drives a big car, gets only ten miles to the gallon."

"Most car owners seem to have trouble getting parts for their motors," said another man. "Nothing fits, they say. But when I need something for my Ford, there's no problem. Every Ford part fits every Ford car."

Finally the experts had to admit they were wrong. Ford's "car for the multitude" really could run. It climbed the steepest hills and plowed through the muddiest roads. It was easy to drive and easy to repair. It cost only $850 and it was inexpensive to operate.

In June of 1909, the Alaska-Yukon-Pacific Exposition, recently opened in Seattle, Washington, announced a transcontinental automobile race. A trophy would be awarded to the car that made the fastest time from New York to Seattle.

Five cars, including two Model T Fords, began the race. The 4,106-mile drive turned out to be a nightmare for the drivers. For most of the way there was no road at all, sometimes not even a marked trail. Rain and hail turned the so-called roads into bogs. Mud often reached up to the axles of the cars.

West of Wyoming the "roads" grew worse and worse. At the summit of the

Cascade Mountains in Washington State, the contestants found deep snow. One of the Fords smashed into a huge rock and was too badly damaged to finish the race.

The driver of the other Model T telegraphed Henry Ford for instructions. Henry had gone to Seattle to be there to welcome the winner.

"Keep coming," Ford wired back. He hired men to shovel snow and took them up the west slope of the Cascades. They dug a path so that the surviving Model T could make it over the mountains.

The sturdy Model T reached Seattle and was proclaimed the winner. It had crossed the continent in 22 days and 55 minutes. The trophy was later withdrawn because of a technicality, but Ford was jubilant. His tough little light-weight car had proved its worth to the world.

9. "Watch the Fords Go By"

Ford's business boomed, but he believed he could double his output. He asked Charles Sorensen, now the plant superintendent, for suggestions.

At that time, two 600-foot avenues stretched through the great Ford factory. Along these paths were 50 stations. At each station two cars could be assembled at a time. Helpers carried necessary parts to the assemblers. It usually took about fourteen hours to assemble a Model T.

"If we could make the chassis move to the parts," Sorensen suggested, "instead of carrying parts to the chassis, we could speed up the assembly process a lot."

One morning in 1913 Sorensen put on a demonstration. Ford and all his staff lined up to watch.

Down one avenue of the big factory came Charlie Sorensen towing a chassis, or frame, with a rope. Six men walked beside the chassis. From piles placed at intervals along the line they picked up parts and attached them to the frame. First came the axles. The wheels followed, then the motor, and so on. Finally the body was added, and the car was finished, ready to be driven out of the plant. The whole process had taken less than six hours.

Ford was delighted. "We've got it now,

Charlie," he said excitedly. "This is the secret of mass production. The work must go to the man, not the man to the work. We'll make a power-driven assembly line and build conveyors to bring parts where they are needed. It will be like a river with many streams flowing into it. No one will have to lift or stoop or walk. We'll turn out twice as many cars, and we'll make twice as much money."

One problem bothered Ford increasingly, however. Assembly-line work was monotonous, uninteresting. The Ford factory had a great turnover of employees, and too much time was wasted in training new men.

One Sunday in January, 1914, Ford called a meeting of some key men in the company. The group included Couzens, Wills, Sorensen, Martin, and Lee.

64

Ford workers (above) assemble the Model T's
electrical system in 1914. Below, a body is
dropped on a chassis to complete a new Ford.

"It's time to talk about wages for the coming year," Ford announced. "Charlie, show us those figures you prepared on production and cost."

Charlie Sorensen wrote some lists of figures on the blackboard.

"It's quite plain," Ford pointed out, "that cost falls as production rises. The more cars we make, the less each car

The Sunday pleasure ride in a Model T was fast becoming an American custom.

costs us. Now suppose we transfer some of our profits to wages, to give our workers an incentive to stay with us?"

Sorensen agreed, but Martin and Couzens did not. Disregarding all protests, Ford indicated the figure of $2 a day, which was then the minimum wage.

"Increase that figure for wages," he directed Sorensen. "Make it $2.50."

When Sorensen had obeyed, Ford said, "Make it $3 . . . $3.50 . . . $4 . . . $4.50."

"You might just as well make it $5," Couzens snapped irritably.

Ford's smile flashed. "That's it!" he exclaimed. "We'll pay our men $5 a day, and we'll reduce the working day to eight hours."

"Why, that policy would bankrupt the company!" Martin protested.

Ford paid no attention to the outraged

grumbling of these opponents. He announced the wage increase the next day.

The news of an eight-hour day at $5, more than double the usual daily wage, electrified the entire nation and the world. Workers stormed Detroit, trying to get jobs with Ford.

Competitors denounced Ford as a madman, a crackpot, and a villain. Other people praised him as a great humanitarian. Both attitudes amused Henry Ford.

"People don't understand," he said to Clara. "I'm not trying to ruin my competitors, and I'm not giving my workers charity. It's just good, sound business to give the employees a share of the profits. They'll work that much harder, and soon they'll be able to buy Ford cars themselves. That will be a whole new market."

10. The Billionaire

Production increased at a rapid rate. In 1915 Ford lowered the price of his touring car to $490 and he sold more cars than ever.

The Model T, affectionately called the "Flivver" or "Tin Lizzie" by its fond owners, soon became the most familiar object on the American scene. Easterners, Westerners, citydwellers, farmers, and townspeople—millions bought Fords. The Model T became as common on the streets of Detroit and other American cities as horses had been when Ford first began his work. Gasoline stations and garages sprang up to service all the cars that swarmed over the country. Streets and roads throughout the nation were soon improved so that automobiles could travel more easily. Of course bad roads and narrow cobblestone streets had never bothered "Tin Lizzie." She could go anywhere and do anything.

Ford jokes began to circulate, and nobody enjoyed them more than Henry Ford. Here are two that were popular:

The man who claims he never gets rattled has never ridden in a Ford.

Question: What shock absorbers does a Model T use?
Answer: The passengers.

College boys put signs on their Fords:

"Danger, 100,000 jolts." "Come, baby, here's your rattle." "Galloping snail."

There were Ford songs too. One of them, called "The Little Ford Rambled Right Along," ended:

Patch it up with a piece of string,
Spearmint gum or any old thing.
When the power gets sick
Just hit it with a brick,
And the little Ford will ramble right along.

Ford had years ago announced that he would no longer build any other car but the Model T. His stockholders objected, but Ford owned more stock than they did, so his decision stood. He built a larger factory so he could turn out more Model T's. The new plant, on the Rouge River between Dearborn and Detroit, was the biggest factory in the United States, if not the world. Both the Rouge and the Highland Park factories were running at full capacity.

As production of "Tin Lizzie" mounted, so did the profits. Ford soon became a millionaire. A few years later he was a billionaire. Still he spent more time at the Ford plants than any of his employees and kept an eye on every detail. He seldom carried any money in his pockets. Sometimes he had to borrow pennies to buy a stamp, or a dollar to pay a restaurant bill.

Now Clara could have everything she wanted, books, music, plenty of shoes for her pretty feet, several luxurious homes, and long trips to Europe. But Edsel, who wanted to go to college when he finished high school, was not so lucky.

"What's the good of college?" his father demanded. "I got along all right without a college education. You go to work in the plant, son."

So Edsel took a job in the Ford factory. On his 21st birthday his father gave him $1,000,000, but Edsel would have preferred a college education.

Money brought troubles, too, the Fords learned. People crowded around the Ford family, all hoping to get something for nothing. Inventors hounded Ford, and so

did job-hunters, salesmen, and beggars. Doorbells and telephones rang constantly. Ford took to climbing in and out of windows to avoid the people at the doors.

"It's got so I can hardly enjoy my garden any more," Clara complained one day. "Someone is always waiting there ready to pounce on me. People have even frightened the birds away from our feeders."

So Ford set guards at the gates of his homes and also his factories. But guards did little good. People climbed fences and hid in shrubbery to catch the Fords. Others waylaid them on the street.

Although Henry Ford had more money now than he knew what to do with, he seldom gave much away. He believed that when a person got something for nothing it made him weak.

Now that Ford was successful, he was also famous. Reporters and photographers followed close on his heels. Everything he said and did was news. After a while Ford came to believe that his ideas and thoughts were more important than those of anyone else in the world. He began to change from a kind, unassuming gentleman who loved birds, children, and practical jokes, to a touchy, unpredictable, intolerant autocrat who gloried in being all powerful. Many men had contributed to Ford's immense success—James Couzens, Harold Wills, William Knudsen, Charles Sorensen, and others. Yet Ford now talked as if he had done it all alone.

In August, 1914, war broke out in Europe. Ford hated war, and he formulated a plan to end the war in Europe. He chartered a ship to take a group of prominent people overseas to talk to rulers of warring nations.

"We'll have the soldiers out of the trenches by Christmas," Ford said.

But the Peace Ship, as it was called, was unsuccessful, and Ford was ridiculed.

In spite of his opposition to war, Ford plunged into war work when the United States entered World War I in April, 1917. He converted his factories to the building of boats, steam turbines, and ambulances—anything needed to help his country win the war. He also built thousands of tractors to speed up farm work, so that the necessary food to feed the people at home and the soldiers abroad could be raised. For these things he was praised.

But Ford used his influence to keep Edsel from being drafted, and for this he was criticized. People protested that it wasn't fair that rich men's sons could stay out of the army while poor men's sons had to fight. Ford told Clara he didn't care what people thought, but he knew Edsel hated his interference.

11. "Henry's Made a Lady out of Lizzie"

The war in Europe ended in November, 1918. The following month Ford, now 55 years old, resigned as president of the Ford Motor Company in favor of his son.

Edsel was now grown, married, and had a son of his own, Henry II. Edsel was a fine, sensitive, intelligent, and capable man, yet he was not allowed to be the real president of the Ford Motor Company.

Like his father before him, Henry Ford expected his son to be like him, to think like him, and to do what he himself would do. He couldn't understand that Edsel was a very different person from himself. So when Edsel made decisions that he didn't agree with, Henry vetoed them. When Edsel signed contracts he didn't like, Henry canceled them.

"I'm president of Ford Motor Company in name only," Edsel told his mother.

Clara knew it was true. Henry would not willingly relinquish his power to anyone else.

One of the chief causes of disagreement between Edsel and Henry was their differing attitudes toward the Model T.

"It's time to bring out a new model, Father," Edsel often urged. "Sales on the Model T are dropping off, and our dealers are begging for a new model."

"The Model T has led the country,

The Ford River Rouge factory is one of the largest industrial plants in the world.

even the world, for years," Henry protested. "It will continue to lead. This is only a temporary slump." He stubbornly refused to consider a new model.

For years Ford had been investing in many different industries. He bought railroads, ships, steel mills, mines, coal fields, timberlands, glass factories, and rubber plantations. Eventually he could produce everything needed to make cars.

All of his life, Ford worked to substitute machine work for handwork, and automobiles for horse travel. Yet he wanted to preserve the past. Near Dearborn he built an early American village called Greenfield, "where people can see how our grandparents lived." He brought back the square dancing and old-time "fiddling" he had loved as a boy. He restored many historic buildings. He rebuilt his father's farmhouse, complete with the dishes his mother had used. He restored the school he had attended as a boy, and even found a stove for it exactly like the one he used to sit in front of when he misbehaved.

Ford also rebuilt Edison's original laboratory. Ever since the great inventor had encouraged him to perfect his gas engine, he had considered Edison one of his best friends. For years Henry Ford, Thomas A. Edison, John Burroughs, the famous naturalist, and Harvey Firestone, maker of Firestone tires, took camping trips together in the summers.

In 1924 many people urged Ford to run for the Presidency of the United States. The idea appealed to him. He believed that the country should be run exactly like a business, and he had no doubt he could run the nation as successfully as he had the Ford Motor Company.

For once Clara did not agree with her husband. Henry would make an efficient dictator, she knew, but not a democratic President. So she spoke her mind:

"The day Mr. Ford runs for President of the United States, that day I will leave for England." Ford did not run.

In May, 1927, the 15,000,000th Ford

came off the assembly line. Conditions in America had changed drastically since the appearance of the first Model T. Dirt roads had given way to concrete, and handwork to factories. Workers now earned far more money and could buy better cars. Only the Ford car remained the same.

At last Henry Ford admitted that the

Henry and Edsel with the new Model A Ford—successor to the long-lived Model T

Model T was outmoded. He closed down his huge factories, and for many months they remained idle during the changeover to the manufacture of a new car.

The Model A was unveiled in December, 1927. The new Ford car created a tremendous sensation. More than 500,000 customers made a down payment on the Model A before they had even seen it. People knew that any car Henry Ford made would be good.

Immediately the newspapers and radio and vaudeville comedians began to joke about Henry Ford's new car. A catch phrase went, "Henry's made a lady out of Lizzie." As always, Ford enjoyed the jokes and the songs, but he was never able to feel the same pride and sense of accomplishment about the Model A that he had felt about the Model T.

12. War with Labor Unions

The years that followed were momentous ones. In 1929 the stock market crashed, bringing ruin to many. The Great Depression followed. Banks closed. Millions of Americans were out of work. Many started selling apples on street corners. Soup kitchens were opened to feed the hungry. Ford sales, like those of other cars, almost ceased.

Franklin D. Roosevelt was elected as President, promising a New Deal to all Americans. Ford bitterly opposed every one of Roosevelt's policies, especially his attempts to regulate business. He refused to sign the government's code of rules for the automobile industry. The government canceled its contracts with the Ford Motor Company. Still Ford wouldn't sign.

"I built my business with my own hands," he fumed, "with my own sweat and my own money. Nobody is going to tell me how to run it, not even the President of the United States."

The government was not the only agency trying to dictate to Henry Ford now. In recent years workers in many industries had joined together to form labor unions. The CIO, a big union made up of many smaller ones, vowed to bring all automobile companies under its control. It intended to set hours, wages, and working conditions.

Ford had no intention of letting the CIO or any other union dictate to him. He instructed his plant guards to keep union organizers away from his employees. The guards now became a factory police force, with Harry Bennett, a former prize fighter, as their leader.

Bennett had no misgivings about using violence to carry out Ford's orders. His guards often followed Ford workers to their homes to be sure they didn't talk to union sympathizers. Ford men caught attending labor meetings were usually beaten up and invariably discharged.

Edsel Ford disapproved of Bennett's strong-arm methods, but his father would not permit him to interfere.

Yet Henry Ford insisted he had nothing to fear from the labor unions. "The union will not succeed in organizing our

men," he declared. "Our workers won't stand for it, I won't stand for it, and the public won't stand for it. Our employees have always been treated fine. They know when they're well off."

However, Ford's union troubles increased. In spite of Bennett and his police, union organizers penetrated the Ford factory. Armed battles broke out

between guards and union men. Finally, in April, 1941, Ford workers went on strike, and the great Ford plant closed. For three months the strike continued.

At last when a vote was taken among Ford employees on the question of joining a union, only about two and a half per cent voted against the union. Ford was furious.

On June 18, 1941, he was handed a union contract. It spelled out the terms on which his men would work, and even set the speed of the assembly line. Ford read it and then stormed out of his office.

"I'm not going to sign that contract," he shouted to Edsel and Sorensen. "I'll close down the plant first."

When he told Clara about his refusal to sign the contract, she was horrified.

"You don't really mean that, Henry!" she cried. "You wouldn't close down the factory!"

"I certainly would," Ford declared. "If the union demands a contract, it's going to find it's dealing with a dark, locked factory."

"But you can't do that," Clara protested. "Think of the men out of work, their families hungry, perhaps homeless.

You have a responsibility to your employees, Henry."

For hours they argued. Ford stuck to his decision stubbornly, but Clara was just as stubborn as he. Finally she announced quietly, "If you refuse to sign that contract, Henry Ford, I'll leave you."

Ford stared incredulously at Clara. For more than 50 years she had been his devoted wife, his companion, his helpmate, his "Great Believer." Life without her was not to be imagined.

"Very well, Callie," he said at last. "I'll sign."

And he did. Not only did he sign, but he gave the union better terms than it asked for. Nobody was going to dictate to Henry Ford. If he had to sign a contract with the union, it was going to be one that he himself dictated.

13. End of an Era

Ford was never the same after that. He was an old man now, and he could not accept changing ways. A few weeks after signing the union contract he had a mild stroke.

In December, 1941, following the Japanese attack on Pearl Harbor, the United States was again plunged into war. Edsel was too old to fight in this war, and he was sick besides. But his son Henry II left his job at the Ford plant and joined the Navy.

Again, in spite of the old man's hatred of war, the Ford Motor Company went into war work. Its factories made B-24's, tractors, tanks, even submarines.

In January Edsel was operated on for stomach ulcers. Henry let no one know how worried he was about his only son. "If the boy would only eat right," he grumbled, "he'd have no trouble with his stomach. Look at me. I'm 78 and strong as a horse. I can run faster, jump farther, and kick higher than anybody on my staff, and I can still chin myself. I never have stomach trouble because I always eat the right foods, and I never drink or smoke." For years Henry Ford had followed one food fad after another. Once it was nuts, another time soy beans. For a while he lived mainly on raw vegetables, especially carrots.

A year later Edsel died of cancer. The shock nearly killed old Henry. Yet he could not bear to give up his hold on the Ford Motor Company. He insisted on being made president of the company again.

Soon Henry II came home from the war and went to work in the plant. He moved into his father's office, and began to acquaint himself with the business.

Henry Ford, seen here at the drawing board, was active in the company until 1945.

Finally in 1945, prodded by Clara, Henry Ford surrendered the presidency of the Ford Motor Company to his eldest grandson, relinquishing all responsibility.

Young Henry's first act as president was to get rid of Harry Bennett and his factory police. The company was soon cleansed of everything that smacked of spying or the use of force on the workers. The Ford Company took on new life.

Henry was almost completely dependent on Clara now. Sick and feeble, he could not bear to have her out of his sight.

In 1947 Henry Ford fell ill and took to his bed. A severe storm had put both electricity and furnace out of service. In Fair Lane, his big cold mansion, which was then lit only by candles, Henry Ford died on April 27, alone with his wife and one servant. He was nearly eighty-four.

After his death, the Ford Foundation was organized to administer his vast fortune. The foundation gives substantial support to various projects in the arts, in medicine, and in other important areas of American life.

Today the Ford car is only one of a great number of automobiles on the highways. Few modern drivers realize that Henry Ford's "car for the multitude" was primarily responsible for the rapid growth of the automobile age. Ford's old "Tin Lizzie" was a pioneer. It ran before there were good roads to run on. It ended the isolation of farmers and did much to unify America. Most of all, it introduced the techniques of mass production to industry.

Ford put the world on wheels, and in so doing, he made it a smaller world.